Volcanoes

by Patricia D. Netzley

**KIDHAVEN
PRESS**™

THOMSON

——————✦——————™

GALE

For Jacob Price, whose love of science is contagious.

On cover: The Kilauea volcano erupts in Hawaii.

For more information, contact
KidHaven Press
27500 Drake Rd.
Farmington Hills, MI 48331-3535
Or you can visit our Internet site at http://www.gale.com

LIBRARY OF CONGRESS CATALOGING-IN-PUBLICATION DATA

Netzley, Patricia D.
    Volcanoes / by Patricia D. Netzley.
        p. cm. — (The KidHaven science library)
    Includes bibliographical references and index.
    Contents: The birth of a volcano—Volcanic eruptions—Active and inactive volca-noes—The damage caused by volcanoes.
    ISBN 0-7377-1391-7 (lib. bdg.: alk. paper)
    1. Volcanoes—Juvenile literature. [1. Volcanoes.] I. Title. II. Series.
    QE521.3.N48 2003
    551.21—dc21
                                        2002008113

Contents

Chapter 1

The Birth of a Volcano

On February 20, 1943, a Mexican farmer noticed something strange in his cornfield. A jagged crack, or **fissure**, had opened up in the earth and was letting off clouds of foul-smelling smoke. By the next day the earth around the fissure had become a cone over thirty feet tall. Named Mount Paricutín after a nearby village, this cone grew in a week to over five hundred feet tall, and within a year it was over twelve hundred feet tall. After nine years Mount Paricutín was almost a mile and a half tall.

Plate Movement

Mount Paricutín's birth was caused by forces deep within the Earth's **mantle**, which is everything beneath the Earth's surface layer, or **crust**, except for the planet's hot center, or **core**. The crust is cracked into fifteen or twenty large sections about sixty miles thick, which are called **tectonic plates**. These plates are always in motion, although they travel slowly.

Scientists disagree on why this movement occurs. Some think that natural forces, perhaps related to magnetism, are pushing or pulling the plates apart. Others believe that the plates are floating or sliding on a layer of rock that is partially or wholly molten. Still others think that the plates are moving on currents of hot air coming up from the core.

Sometimes two plates bump into each other. When this happens the lighter of the two plates is usually driven under the heavier one, causing cracks to form in the mantle. Eventually these cracks create openings called **volcanoes** that allow **magma**, a hot (over 2012°F or 1100°C) mixture of molten rock and gases, to rise out of Earth's interior.

Volcanoes form when two tectonic plates slide into each other.

In most cases, the lighter plate is carrying oceanic crust (crust under an ocean). The plate that remains on the surface is carrying continental crust (crust under a land mass). Therefore, most volcanoes are born near places where ocean and land meet. In fact, over 75 percent of the world's volcanoes circle the plate that carries the Pacific Ocean, making a ring of volcanoes called the Ring of Fire.

Magma Formation

Scientists disagree on what makes volcanoes form in places where one plate goes under another. Years ago, scientists thought that magma existed throughout the mantle and could break through the crust at any location. Now, however, most scientists believe that the movement of one plate beneath another creates magma somewhere between fifteen and one hundred miles below the Earth's surface. They disagree, however, on how this happens.

A few scientists think that the rubbing of one plate against another creates heat deep within the mantle, melting the surrounding rock to make magma. Most scientists, however, believe that the downward-moving plate carries seawater and minerals from the ocean floor into the mantle, and that it is these materials that melt the rock. Indeed, some of the most common substances in ocean sediment are carbon dioxide, sodium, and potassium. These can lower the melting temperature of

Ring of Fire

Asia

North America

Hawaii

Pacific Ocean

South America

Australia

● Volcanoes

rock. Another such substance, carbonate, can increase the amount of gases already within the magma when mixed with saltwater.

Once a certain amount of magma has formed within the mantle, it rises towards the crust. Some scientists think this upward movement is triggered by the gases within the magma. These gases include carbon dioxide, hydrogen, carbon monoxide, and sulfur dioxide. They think that as the magma increases in volume, its heat and gases increase and its density, or solidity, decreases. Once it has become much less dense than the surrounding rock, it rises. Other scientists, however, believe that plate movement causes the magma to rise. Something similar happens when a person shakes a can of soda pop. The soda contains carbon dioxide gas. When the soda is shaken, it erupts. As with soda, magma erupts through a sudden opening in the Earth's crust after being shaken by the forces of moving plates.

The Magma Chamber

As the magma rises, the pressure caused by its gases can force the earth around it to balloon outwards. This creates a pocket known as a **magma chamber**. Within this chamber the magma melts the surrounding rock and becomes more and more gaseous. When the magma puts enough pressure on the crust above, the chamber cracks. A volcano is created. This **vent**, or pathway to the surface, allows the magma's gases and steam to escape the earth, reducing its pressure.

If the pressure falls to a certain level, the magma stops rising. This happens about 90 percent of the time. The magma remains in its magma chamber, goes only partway up the vent, or stops near the top of the vent. The remaining 10 percent of the time, the pressure in the magma is still high enough to push it up and out of the volcano. Once this occurs, the magma is known as **lava**.

For nine years, Mount Paricutín had many eruptions of lava and rock fragments. As these materials spilled out over the mountain's sides, they created a small cone that grew larger with each eruption. Most volcanoes develop in this way, ending up as volcanic mountains with steep sides and one central vent, and possibly also one or more small side vents where steam and gas can escape. These volcanic mountains are called **strato volcanoes**.

Strato volcanoes with cone-shaped peaks are called cones. Cones under fifteen hundred feet tall, like Mount Paricutín, are called cinder cones. Those over fifteen hundred feet tall, such as Mount Saint Helens in Washington, are called composite cones. This is because their sides usually have been built up through eruptions of both lava and ash. ("Composite" means a combination of different materials.) Strato volcanoes with slightly rounded peaks, such as Mount Lassen in California, are called lava domes.

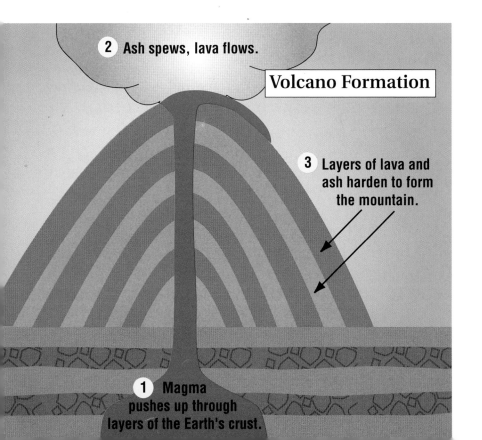

2 Ash spews, lava flows.

Volcano Formation

3 Layers of lava and ash harden to form the mountain.

1 Magma pushes up through layers of the Earth's crust.

Volcanic mountains whose sides are low and gently sloped rather than steep are called **shield volcanoes**, because they look like a warrior's shield lying on the ground. Shield volcanoes have several large vents, all of them allowing lava to flow down the sides of the volcanic mountain. One example of this type of volcano is Kilauea in Hawaii. Like most shield volcanoes, Kilauea erupts frequently but not explosively. The sides of such a volcano often swell just before an eruption as magma presses up from below, and then lava oozes out of many or all of the volcano's vents.

A third type of volcano is the **seamount**, or underwater volcano. These volcanoes have puffy sides because the ocean cools and hardens the lava's outer skin while its insides are still expanding and bubbling with gases. This type of lava is called pillow lava.

Persistent Magma

Sometimes the lava coming out of a volcano becomes blocked. This most commonly happens with seamounts and shield volcanoes that have formed within plates rather than at plate edges. When the plate carrying one of these formations moves the volcano away from the "hot spot" where the magma is rising, the magma no longer has a way to escape. This means that it can no longer continue erupting until it punches a new hole in

The cone shape at the top of a volcano (left) points toward the sky.

A chain of volcanoes is sometimes created when plates move and the flow of magma to the earth's surface is blocked.

the crust next to the old one. If the plate continues to shift, a chain of volcanoes can be created over time. Scientists disagree on what might cause magma to rise in the middle of a plate. They know, however, that less than 5 percent of the world's volcanoes were created this way.

Fissures and volcanic cones can also become blocked when the leading edge of the lava coming out of them cools before it can flow too far. The cooled lava then acts as a dam, so that the rest of the magma cannot come out. However, the magma usually bursts through the dam or creates another fissure nearby. This happens because once magma forms it continues to seek ways to release its heat and gases up and out of the earth, sometimes erupting with great force to unplug a vent.

Chapter 2

Volcanic Eruptions

In January 1973 Heimaey Island in Iceland began having small earthquakes that opened several fissures in the ground, some of them two miles long. These fissures then began spitting out lava, sometimes throwing balls of it high into the air, and within a few days one fissure had created a volcanic cone over three hundred feet high. This cone, named Eldfell ("Fire Mountain"), soon produced a lava flow that traveled at a rate of over fifteen hundred cubic feet per second.

When people in the island town of Vestmannaeyjar realized that the lava flow was heading for their town, they pumped seawater onto the lava to cool and harden it, first at a rate of five hundred tons of water an hour and later at two hundred thousand tons an hour. By April these efforts had turned the leading edge of the flow into a dam that diverted the remaining lava away from the village. However, dozens of homes had been lost by this time. Meanwhile, Eldfell had begun to collapse, and by summer it had stopped erupting.

Many similar volcanoes have formed in Iceland, because in this area, called a **rift zone**, two of the plates carrying the Earth's crust are pulling apart. Some scientists believe that as these two plates pull apart, the energy they create somehow causes magma to form beneath the surface and come out through the gap between the plates. Other scientists believe that the plates are pulling apart because the magma is already underneath them, putting pressure on them to separate so it can

A volcano throws lava and smoke into the air above the town of Vestmannaeyjar in Iceland.

come out. In either case, the plates never truly separate, because the magma coming through the gap fills the space between the plates with new crust.

Eruptions of Lava

All of Iceland's volcanoes give off large amounts of lava, but the lava usually flows slowly because it is thick, and thick liquids move slower than thin liquids. The thickness of any lava is determined by what kind of rock the lava is made of. For example, lava that comes from basalt, a heavy black rock, is thin and runny. This is the type of lava in Hawaiian eruptions. Icelandic lava, however, is made of rhyolite, a pale granite that becomes thick and sticky when it melts.

The force with which lava is ejected from the volcano depends on how much gas is in the magma as it reaches the volcano's vent. When much of its gas has escaped on the way up, the lava oozes quietly from the volcano. Lava that is highly gaseous can explode into the air as high as one hundred thousand feet. Since thin lava releases gases more easily than thick lava, Hawaiian volcanoes have the calmest eruptions of lava, while Icelandic eruptions can have great force.

Such forceful eruptions can spit balls of lava, called **lava bombs**, into the air. Different types of lava bombs have different names depending on their shape. For example, breadcrust bombs are bombs of sticky lava that form a crust as they fly through the air, while ribbon bombs are thick strands of lava that twist and harden as they fly.

Lava bombs occur during powerful volcanic eruptions.

Some lava bombs are fairly small, while others are bigger than a person and might weigh over a ton.

Rocks and Steam

Rock fragments ejected from a volcano are called **tephra**. Large chunks of ejected rock are called bombs, medium ones lapilli, and very small ones ash and dust. Most bombs are the size of a baseball or basketball, although some might be more than four feet across and weigh one hundred tons. The rock fragments that make up ash are no more than one fifth of an inch in diameter, while those in dust are less than four hundredths of an inch in diameter.

All tephra is made from sticky magma because of the large amount of gas trapped in it. When the gas explodes as it leaves the vent, it blows the magma into fragments that cool in the air to become tephra.

Two other substances to come out of a volcano during an eruption are **pumice** and steam. Pumice is a natural glass that comes from lava. It is light-weight and has holes in it because of gas bubbles that were present in the rock before it cooled. Steam can come either from the magma inside the volcano or from hot water within nearby rocks.

Over 90 percent of all eruptions involve gas, steam, and solid material but no magma, because the erupting gases have released so much pressure that the magma no longer has enough force to erupt. For example, in March 1980 Mount Saint Helens in Washington State started steaming because magma was heating water in the volcano's vent. One month later the volcano's north side began to bulge, and on May 18, 1980, the bulge exploded, but no magma came out. Instead the volcano released a cloud of fiery gases, volcanic ash, and pieces of rock, followed by several more such clouds.

Pyroclastic Flows

Avalanches of fiery gases, ash, and rocks are called **pyroclastic flows**. Some scientists think that they happen because an erupting volcano's vent has become clogged, forcing the volcano to explode gases out its side instead of its top, just as Mount Saint Helens did. Other scientists, however, think that such flows occur whenever an eruption's gases are too heavy to shoot up into the air.

As it travels down a mountainside, a pyroclastic flow usually divides into two parts. One part is a cloud of gases mixed with pebbles, dust, and ash that moves as fast as 185 miles per hour. The other part is a mass of heavier rocks that moves more slowly along the ground. The slower part is usually hotter than the faster part. For example, in the Mount Vesuvius eruption, of A.D. 79, modern-day scientists determined the faster part of the flow was 212°F (100°C), while the slower part was 752°F (400°C).

Types of Eruptions

Eruptions that include a pyroclastic flow are called Peléan eruptions. This name comes from the West Indies volcano of Mount Pelée, whose eruption of pyroclastic flows in 1902 killed nearly forty thousand people. Peléan eruptions involve sticky lava with lots of gases and are so violent that they usually blow apart most or all of the volcano.

Plinean eruptions, named for the philosopher Pliny the Elder who died in the A.D. 79 eruption of Mount Vesuvius, are very violent eruptions that explode upward, sending huge amounts of tephra and other volcanic materials into the air. For example, the A.D. 79 Mount Vesuvius eruption spit

Fire and ash pour out of Mount Saint Helens.

Volcanic explosions are often part of extremely violent eruptions.

out one cubic mile of tephra over a two-day period. Slightly less violent are Vesuvian eruptions, named after eruptions of Mount Vesuvius after A.D. 79, and Vulcanean eruptions, named after Mount Vulcano in Italy. They too blow volcanic materials into the air but are not as explosive as Plinean eruptions and do not produce as much material.

Strombolian Eruptions

The next most violent eruption is a Strombolian eruption, named after another Italian volcano. This type of eruption has short, small explosions that bubble lava into the air and produces a lot of gas and steam. Most of this lava remains near the volcano's vent. Icelandic eruptions also have small explosions, but their lava tends to flow far away from the vent. Lava flows are a part of Hawaiian eruptions as well, but these eruptions usually do not involve explosions because Hawaiian lava is very thin and has little gas.

Scientists have developed these labels to group eruptions by type, but they sometimes find it difficult to place an eruption into any particular category. No two volcanoes behave in exactly the same way, even when they have been formed under the same conditions. In addition, one volcano might erupt with different levels of force at different times.

Chapter 3

Active and Inactive Volcanoes

There are about 1500 active volcanoes on Earth today, over 65 of them in the United States. However, when scientists say that a volcano is active, they mean that it could erupt at any time, not necessarily that it is in the process of erupting. Between 850 and 1500 volcanoes have erupted during the past 10,000 years, but no more than 25 volcanoes usually erupt in any one year. However, at any particular moment there are 8 to 12 volcanoes erupting at various places throughout the world, either on land or underwater.

Dormant Volcanoes

Some active volcanoes have long periods of activity. For example, Mount Izalco in South America has been considered active ever since it first erupted in 1770. However, other active volcanoes have gone through long dormant, or quiet, periods, when they appear to have lost the ability to erupt.

For example, Mount Saint Helens had a dormant period of 123 years before its 1980 eruption. Mount Pinatubo in the Philippines had a dormant period of six centuries before it erupted in 1991.

During dormant periods, many volcanoes continue to let off steam because of the magma still inside the volcano. In addition, lava may continue to boil in the volcano's **crater**, a bowl-shaped area that appears around the opening of most volcanic vents. Craters are caused by molten rock ejected through the vent, which can create a lava lake that shapes the crater. Sometimes during a dormant period, this lake cools and hardens, creating a plug over the vent. Pressure then builds up beneath the plug, so that when the volcano erupts again its explosion is especially huge.

Craters form when molten rock is pushed through a volcano's vent.

Calderas

Sometimes an eruption is so forceful that it destroys the volcano that produced it. For example, when Mount Mazama erupted approximately six thousand years ago in southwestern Oregon, the volcano was completely destroyed, leaving behind a deep depression called a **caldera** (from the Spanish word for cauldron, a cooking pot). When scientists see a caldera, they know that a volcano was once there.

A caldera is created from a volcano's crater. When a massive explosion takes place inside the volcano, the tall sides of a crater collapse and flatten into the wider bowl of a caldera. Many of these depressions are big, because the volcanoes that create them

Crater Lake in Oregon was created seventy-seven hundred years ago.

tend to be big. For example, the caldera created by the eruption of Mount Mazama is over six miles wide and two thousand feet deep, and from these measurements scientists can tell that the volcano was once at least twelve thousand feet high. A body of water called Crater Lake now fills the caldera.

Other calderas have created a ring of islands. For example, the Greek islands of Thera, Therasia, and Aspronisi are actually parts of the rim of a large underwater caldera caused by a volcanic explosion over thirty-five hundred years ago. This caldera is approximately four by seven miles in size, with a depth of more than one thousand feet and sides taller than thirteen hundred feet in several places. In the middle of the caldera a new volcano is beginning to form, because magma is still being produced beneath the water.

Similarly, when the Indonesian volcano of Krakatau erupted in 1883, it created a caldera beneath the sea about four miles in diameter, and a new volcano began to form there in 1927. This new volcano, called Anak Krakatau or "child of Krakatau," rose above the surface of the ocean to create a small island in 1930 and it remains active today, sometimes letting off plumes of steam and ash.

Magma Levels

A caldera also can be formed when the level of magma in a magma chamber drops. This happens

From a small boat, Anak Krakatau can be seen spewing steam and ash.

either because magma is being erupted out of the volcano faster than the chamber can refill or because the volcano did not make new magma after its last eruption. In either case, without magma to support it, the chamber's ceiling can collapse into a caldera.

Evidence of this process can be seen in the Hawaiian volcano Kilauea, which has a caldera that changes in size and depth depending on the levels of magma within the volcano. Sometimes magma pushes up to raise the floor of the volcano's caldera and fill it with lava. Other times magma leaks out through nearby fissures, dropping the level of the caldera's floor by several feet and draining its lava lake.

Sometimes a rising caldera floor is evidence that a dormant volcano is about to erupt. For example, in 1980 the floor of the Long Valley Caldera of California, which is a depression about nine miles

Hot lava leaks from the surface of Kilauea in Hawaii.

by nineteen miles in size near Mammoth Mountain, rose twenty-five inches. Therefore, scientists think that a magma chamber beneath the area is beginning to fill.

Inactive Volcanoes

Until recently, scientists thought that Mammoth Mountain was an inactive volcano. Now they know that it is just dormant, because inactive volcanoes no longer produce magma. Inactive volcanoes also no longer give off any heat, whereas a dormant volcano might have hot springs or other areas of hot water and steam that show there is still magma underground. However, since hot springs can also appear in areas where there are no volcanoes (although scientists do not understand why), their presence does not prove that an active or dormant volcano is nearby. In fact, it is so hard to tell whether a volcano is inactive that some scientists believe all volcanoes that have erupted within the past ten thousand years should be considered active.

Volcanoes that do seem to be in the process of becoming inactive usually have a period of cooling down called the **fumarolic stage**. (The word *fumarole* comes from the Italian word for "giving off fumes.") During this stage, which begins after the volcano has stopped erupting either lava or tephra, the volcano continues to give off hot steam and gases, but these gradually get cooler and smaller in

A geyser jets water and steam from below the earth's crust.

amount. As part of this process, hot water might also erupt from the volcano as **geysers**, which are jets of water and steam.

If the volcano truly has become inactive and not just dormant, it will get smaller as time passes. It shrinks because stream water, rainwater, wind, and other forces wear down its sides over a period of

Lava tubes push through an underground volcanic chamber.

many years. This process is called erosion. Sometimes erosion wears away parts of the volcano to create interesting rock formations. For example, erosion might leave only a volcano's central vent, a tube of rock called a volcanic pipe.

Other times erosion wears away all of the volcano, and people build towns on the spot where it once stood. Then the only evidence that a volcano was once there might be a hardened lava flow or other lava formation nearby. One of the most interesting of these formations is a lava tube, which is made when the outside of a stream of lava hardens while its insides continue to flow. People can actually walk through lava tubes, some of which are a mile long.

Devil's Post Pile

Another interesting lava formation is Devil's Post Pile in California, near Mammoth Mountain. About nine thousand years ago a lava flow in this area cracked as it cooled, creating thick posts that now look like they are made of wood. Some of these posts are sixty feet high, while others are broken and lying jumbled on the ground. Such formations are the most harmless aftereffects of a volcanic eruption; the ash and gas can cause problems for years after the volcano has become dormant or inactive.

Chapter 4

The Damage Caused by Volcanoes

After the Indonesian volcano of Krakatau erupted with a series of explosions in 1883, a final blast blew up two-thirds of the volcanic island and collapsed it into the sea. This event, along with several pyroclastic flows produced earlier, created ocean waves that were over fifty feet high and traveled great distances, destroying ships at sea and plants, animals, and people on nearby islands. Meanwhile the coast of Sumatra was struck by a hot cloud of volcanic ash and steam that traveled across the surface of the ocean and burned thousands of people to death.

The number of people killed during the Krakatau eruption was between forty thousand and ninety-six thousand, with most of the bodies being washed out to sea. These bodies, along with material ejected from the volcano, clogged the waters around Indonesia's islands, and over the next year the ocean's currents carried some of the volcanic material as far away as the eastern coastline of

Africa. However, many of the bodies of people killed in the eruption were never found.

Loss of Life

Most deaths from volcanic eruptions are caused by fiery gases and ash rather than lava. For example, during the 1980 Mount Saint Helens eruption, which ejected about 275 million tons of material into the air, over 50 people died from breathing in ash instead of air. During the A.D. 79 eruption of Mount Vesuvius, the ash from pyroclastic flows buried the towns of Herculaneum and Pompeii and killed approximately 16,000 people. In the 1902 eruption of Mount Pelée, almost 30,000 people were killed by a pyroclastic

A victim of the Pompeii disaster lies in a layer of hardened ash many centuries after the volcanic eruption.

flow with a temperature of over 1800°F (1000°C) that traveled about 95 miles an hour. Such events also destroy plants, including valuable food crops.

Pyroclastic flows can also cause mudslides that damage the landscape. For example, when the 1980 Mount Saint Helens eruption let loose its first pyroclastic flow, it caused an avalanche of rocks, snow, and ice that felled every tree in its path. The rest of its pyroclastic flows melted snow and ice on the mountain, which caused massive mudslides that removed most remaining plants and topsoil. The worst such disaster, however, took place in Colombia in 1985, when a mudflow after the eruption of the Nevado del Ruiz volcano killed twenty-two thousand people.

Bad Air

Volcanic eruptions can also pose a great risk to people flying planes nearby, because when airplane engines suck in ash and smoke they can fail. For example, during the 1989–1990 eruption of the Redoubt Volcano in Alaska, one jumbo jet carrying 244 passengers lost the use of one of its engines after flying near the volcano and almost crashed. Other volcanic eruptions in Alaska, such as that of Mount Spurr in 1992 and Mount Pavlof in 1996, have caused similar problems.

Another serious threat to human health comes when a volcano ejects large amounts of sulfur gases into the air. For example, when Mount

The eruption of Nevado del Ruiz in Colombia in 1985 caused a mudslide that killed twenty-two thousand people.

Pinatubo erupted in the Philippines in 1991, it ejected 15 to 20 million tons of sulfur dioxide gas into the air, along with several 130-mile-wide ash clouds. This gas then combined with hydrogen in the atmosphere to produce small drops of sulfuric acid. Some of these drops later fell to Earth as acid rain, a polluted rainwater that can destroy plants and cause serious illnesses in human beings.

Some of the sulfuric acid from the Pinatubo eruption formed a cloud that spread around the world over the next three weeks. It took several years for this cloud to disappear. Similarly, the eruption of Krakatau produced volcanic dust that not only fell as far as fifteen hundred miles away but stayed in the atmosphere for years.

Problems in the Atmosphere

Scientists have discovered that volcanic dust blown high into the air can end up in three different levels of the atmosphere. The lowest level is the troposphere, about nine miles up. Any dust that lands here will soon come down as rain. The highest level is the mesosphere, over thirty miles up. Any dust that lands here will create big, thin clouds that may cause storms. In between these two levels is the stratosphere, about twelve to fifteen miles up. Dust that lands here has the most serious effect on Earth's climate, because it can drift across the planet to create a curtain between the Earth and the sun, blocking out light and heat. Sulfuric acid droplets also keep sunlight from reaching Earth, by reflecting light back towards the sun.

Therefore, major eruptions can affect Earth's climate. For example, the Pinatubo eruption dropped the average temperature of the Earth by about 39°F (1°C) for several years. The 1815 eruption of an Indonesian volcano named Tambora, which ejected over one hundred times the material of the Mount Saint Helens eruption, brought several years of colder weather throughout the world. In fact, the year after Tambora erupted, 1816, there was no warmth that summer.

During prehistoric times, an Indonesian volcano called Toba ejected so much volcanic material—perhaps enough to cover well over a thousand miles in all directions—that it probably lowered global temperatures by over 50°F (10°C). Since this happened at a time when the Earth was already

Volcanic Eruptions and the Atmosphere

Mesosphere: Dust creates thin clouds that can cause storms.

Stratosphere: Dust blocks light and heat.

Troposphere: Dust returns to earth with rain.

going through a period of cold called the Ice Age, it surely caused great suffering among early humans. In fact, some scientists believe that this event nearly made humans extinct.

Dangerous Neighbors

Not everything about volcanoes is bad. Eruptions can create new crust for Earth and bring metals and minerals, like gold, to the surface for mining. Some of these minerals are also carried within volcanic steam up into the atmosphere. Later they are deposited in the Earth's oceans, where they help certain sea creatures survive, or on land, where they fertilize soil.

Another benefit of volcanoes is the heat that they can produce. Volcanic hot springs and steam can be used to run power plants that make electricity. In fact, Italy has been making electricity from volcanic steam since 1904, and Iceland has been using it to heat homes for over seventy years. The state of California has been using **geothermal energy**—heat from the Earth—for about fifty years to provide electricity to some of its major cities, including San Francisco.

But although volcanoes do offer some benefits, they are still dangerous neighbors. Volcanoes can become active with very little warning, and scientists have trouble predicting which dormant or seemingly inactive volcanoes might suddenly come to life. In fact, even after a volcano shows signs that it might soon erupt, scientists cannot tell

Mines are often the sites where volcanic eruptions have brought precious metals to the earth's surface.

exactly when or even if this eruption will happen. Scientists also cannot predict when a volcano might cause an earthquake or a landslide.

The science of volcanoes, called vulcanology, will surely make great strides in the future. In fact,

A vulcanologist studies volcanic activity in hopes of preventing disasters.

scientists have already developed ways to check for warning signs of an eruption, monitoring earthquake activity and the presence of heat and certain gases. Such efforts helped save lives when scientists successfully predicted the eruption of Mount Pinatubo and evacuated over eighty-five thousand people in the area before the blast. However, sometimes such predictions are wrong, and it is not possible to monitor every volcano given the expense that such efforts involve. Therefore it will always be risky for people to live in areas where the Earth creates volcanoes.

caldera: A large depression formed when a volcanic crater collapses.

core: The hot center of the Earth, an area that some scientists think is liquid and others solid or semi-solid.

crater: A bowl-shaped area that forms around the vent of a volcanic mountain.

crust: The outer layer of Earth's rock, which is covered with soil.

fissure: A jagged crack in Earth's crust, caused by earthquakes, volcanic activity, and plate movement.

fumarolic stage: A period when a volcano appears to be cooling down, during which it releases steam and/or gas.

geothermal energy: Heat produced by the Earth.

geyser: A jet of water from inside the Earth, heated and shot into the air by forces within magma.

lava: The term for magma when it is on Earth's surface.

lava bombs: Balls of lava that shoot up into the air and rain down on nearby lands during an eruption.

magma: A hot liquid of molten rock and gases, made within the Earth at a depth of anywhere from fifteen to one hundred miles.

magma chamber: The area at the bottom of a volcanic vent that is filled with magma prior to an eruption.

mantle: The large area of the Earth between the crust and the core.

pumice: A lightweight volcanic rock, actually a natural glass, with many holes.

pyroclastic flows: Clouds of gas and volcanic debris that travel along the ground rather than up into the air.

rift zone: An area where two tectonic plates are separating and new crust is being formed from rising magma.

seamount: An underwater volcano.

shield volcanoes: Volcanoes with gentle slopes made by lava flowing fairly quietly from many vents.

strato volcanoes: Volcanic mountains with steep, high sides and a central vent, although lava might also escape from the mountain through small fissures in the mountainside as well.

tectonic plates: Segments of Earth's crust and upper edge of the mantle.

tephra: Rock fragments of various sizes ejected from a volcano during an eruption.

vent: A pathway inside a volcano by which magma travels to the surface. A volcano may have many vents.

volcano: An opening in the earth's crust and surface through which magma, gases, steam, tephra, and other substances from inside the earth can escape with varying degrees of force.

Books

Robert Decker and Barbara Decker, *Volcanoes.* New York: W.H. Freeman, 1999. For more advanced readers, this book provides clear, detailed information related to the science of vulcanology. It also discusses how volcanoes form and provides examples of volcanic eruptions throughout history.

Jeff Groman, *The Atlas of Natural Disasters.* New York: Friedman/Fairfax, 2000. This book gives details about many natural disasters, including major volcanic eruptions.

Matthys Levy and M.G. Salvadori, *Why the Earth Quakes: The Story of Earthquakes and Volcanoes.* New York: W.W. Norton, 1995. This book describes the relationships between tectonic plates and volcanoes and tells about famous eruptions.

Ellen Thro, *Volcanoes of the United States.* New York: Franklin Watts, 1992. This book provides information on volcanoes throughout the United States, as well as on hot springs, geothermal power, and the science of vulcanology.

Gregory Vogt, *Predicting Volcanic Eruptions.* New York: Franklin Watts, 1989. This book describes scientists' efforts to predict when certain volcanoes will erupt.

Websites

Annenberg/CPB Learner.org (www.learner.org). Maintained by the Annenberg/CPB Channel, a satellite channel for schools, this website discusses the science of vulcanology and scientists' efforts to predict volcanic eruptions.

Volcanoes.com (www.volcanoes.com). This website provides a lot of current information about volcanoes around the world as well as about books and videos related to volcanoes.

Volcano World (http://volcano.und.nodak.edu). Maintained by the University of North Dakota, this website provides information about current volcanic eruptions as well as many interesting facts about volcanoes.

Index

Picture Credits

Cover photo: © Jack Fields/Photo Researchers
© Bettmann/CORBIS, 14
© Corel Corporation, 27
© Tony Craddock/SPL/Photo Researchers, Inc., 24
© Sergio Dorantes/CORBIS, 26
© Simon Fraser/Science Photo Library/Photo
   Researchers, 29
© Langevin Jacques/CORBIS SYGMA, 35
Chris Jouan, 37
© John Mead/SPL/Photo Researchers, Inc., 39
National Oceanic and Atmospheric Association, 5,
   10, 12, 16, 20
Brandy Noon, 7, 9
© John Reader/Science Photo Library, 23
© Roger Ressmeyer/CORBIS, 30, 33
U.S. Geological Survey, 40
© D. Weintraub/Photo Researchers, 19

About the Author

Patricia D. Netzley is the author of dozens of books for children, young adults, and adults. Her nonfiction books include *The Stone Age, The Encyclopedia of Environmental Literature, The Curse of King Tut, Haunted Houses, Life on an Everest Expedition, The Encyclopedia of Women's Travel and Exploration, The Encyclopedia of Movie Special Effects,* and *The Encyclopedia of Witchcraft.*